AF665404

The self-defence mini handbook

By: Ivehag

Adam Ivehag

Author and Mensa member, who among other things studied:
Myology, Osteology and Physiology.
By TA ESD Certified Self-defence coach. (KMA/IKMF P1.)

I have a wide range of interests and hobbies and in this manual I intend to share a little bit about one of them, self-defence. An interest starting in practice with some Judo classes and reading Viking Cronholm's booklet Jiujiutsu tricks (released in 1908) as a kid. Then it continued in high school with a P1 (Yellow belt) after a season of IKMF style Krav Maga at a KMA school until it closed. After that I wanted to learn more and purchased a pile of books to start learning including but not limited to the three manuals: Savate Assaut & Combat. Ju-jutsu (the instruction book for Jujutsu Kai, a style influenced by Durewall Jiujiutsu a style that began with the very same booklet I once read), and Complete Krav Maga by Darren Levine and John Witman with foreword by former MMA Champion Bass Rutten. I then proceeded to practice with friends and family, including after a request from my mother practicing techniques from the Krav Maga book with her for a year and testing techniques with my father whom you will read about on the next page, and carried on from there.

Bernt Ivehag

Also starting with Judo in younger days (Blue belt), he has an interest in weapon techniques.

My father went on to join the Swedish army and serve two tours in Bosnia, two tours in Kosovo and one tour in Afghanistan.

In that time, he worked both with the UN, IFOR, and KFOR etc.

He also served in the home guard a long time.

His role was driver of the 302 APC (and later on Transporter (Car) and Medic.)

His weapon training includes but is not limited to: AK4, AK5,AKAN, KSP Machinegun, Glock (Pistol 88), various Grenades, Pepper spray and Baton.

He is currently retired from the military

but occasionally active in the home guard.

(Guest star: Gucci the little dog)

In this book you will learn a few basic methods of self-defence.

Self-defence is not the same thing as a martial arts (arts of war sometimes including the use of traditional or modern weapons and often with religious components) or combat sports where one dedicates a large portion of life, risks a variety of serious injuries such as CTE, joint damage, as well as other serious impact or long-term injuries and practices for years to be champion.

If someone is looking for something to practice a short time in order to prevent injury and has no intention to compete, this matches poorly. Other reasons may be: Limited education time, Religious or Philosophical reasons or Health reasons etc.

What would you teach a security guard, police officer, soldier or civilian if I gave you perhaps just a few days or weeks?

The result is hopefully the appropriate design of a self-defence course.

Self-defence is two things.

First, as a system/course it is something designed to be:

A. Simple, using heavy motor skills.

B. Be useable by a non-athlete and

C. Quick and easy to learn and Functional with relatively little practice.

(Thus suitable for people with limited training time such as security guards, police, and soldiers, etc)

This mini-book is designed for civilian one and two day courses. The focus is on getting away.

Second, it is a legal term. To be self-defence it:

A. Needs to be in response to an attack or immediate threat of attack.

B. Can not be a revenge action such as following someone who hit you earlier to hit them now and

C. The use of force must be reasonable in proportion to the threat

*Not legal advice, learn your local laws

Notes

Learning self-defence doesn't make you Rambo.

Your actions are solely your own responsibility.

That includes the safety of your practice partner.

Some techniques may not well suited to you as a person here or elsewhere. Practise with resistance to make sure the move works for you.

Always remember, he who becomes the very thing he has fought has truly suffered final defeat.

If your strategy is to run, can you actually outrun the attacker? Practice sprints, long-distance running and obstacle courses. (Also learn a few techniques on how to get out of attempts to grab or hold you down, (like in this booklet) and consider a few good escape routes in advance)

Self-defence weapons :

If available things like Guns, Knives, Tasers etc are useful.

However, in many places such are illegal, in those places the following may be allowed: Sturdy walking stick, Self-defence spray, metal pen, Personal alarm etc. Learn your local laws.

(Keep in mind that weapons you bring but are not proficient with may be used against you.)

(I will not be sharing armed techniques in this particular manual)

Principles

Hand to hand.

Your first line of defence is to avoid danger.

Walk with confidence, bring friends, take a safer route, run away,

and you may arm yourself in accordance with what the laws in your country allow.

Second is de-escalation, when possible, talk to the person as if their friend and try to make them rethink the situation.

(But be careful not to come off romantic or condescending)

Third is active defence, strike hard and fast, apply the appropriate technique and get away.

We mustn't act as if the world was as we wished it were, but as it actually is.

Once running try to break the line of sight and "disappear".

Perhaps get lost among the shelves of a store or sneak into the personnel only area and ask for help. If there are security guards contact them, if there is a police station nearby run into it.

Sticks

Close the distance fast and suddenly.

Keep your arms at an angle to prevent breaking them.

(A note on training: Use a lightweight stick, preferably covered in foam, for a high-paced yet safe training.)

Guns

Redirect.

Secure.

Disarm.

(A note on training: Be careful about your finger on the trigger especially when performing the long gun defence, as the finger can be injured. Always wear safety gear and give the simple command "Shoot me if you see me go for the gun" if practicing with a soft air gun for a realistic yet safe practice.)

Knives

Strong and determined techniques to create space and if lucky knock out or knock down the attacker.

Keep the space by kicks to belly, liver or groin. (and if available using nearby object such as a chair, pool cue or door. Perhaps a sharp object of your own depending on your surroundings) Escape when possible. (A note on training: practice parrying the knife using a fake knife or object of similar size. Never practice with a real knife) Also remember, in real life there are many variables and many things that can go wrong, try to avoid unnecessary risks. Never underestimate the danger of a knife.

Index

Defences:

1. Wrist release, one handed (Upwards)

2. Wrist release, one handed (Downwards)

3. Wrist release, two handed

4. Standing elbow lock

5. Strangle defence front

6. Strangle defence rear

7. Front break fall.

8. Back break fall

9. Side break fall

10. Hip throw

11. Ground mount escape.

12. Ground strangle defence

13. Ground between the knees escape

14. Ground defence position

Strikes:

15. Palm strike from active guard. (With or without eye poke and groin kick)

16. Defensive Front Kick

Weapons:

17. Stick. Vertical Inside “Dive” Defence

18. Stick. Horizontal “Guard” Defence

19. Stick. Vertical Outside “X” Defence

20. Knife. The 360 technique

21. Knife. Folds

22. Knife. Standing elbow lock

23. Gun. Long front defence

24. Gun. Short front defence

25. Gun. Quick front defence

26. Gun. Back defence

1. Wrist releases one handed (Upwards)

("Wrist Release Two Hands Held Down" from the KMW Krav Maga Yellow belt curriculum. IKMF "Two hands grabbing two hands low" P3 Curriculum) This technique is useful against wrist grabs of both one and two arms.

If your wrist is grabbed in a lower position, simply bring the wrist up as to a guard in a sharp manner. The mechanical principle is to break out of the grab towards the top of the attackers thumb.

2. Wrist release (Downwards)

("Wrist Release: Two Hands Held High" from KMW Krav Maga Yellow belt curriculum. "One hand grabbing one hand, high hold across" from IKMF Krav Maga P3 Curriculum)

This technique can as the previous be applied on either one or two wrists, as well as in a tighter motion (like IKMF).

Bring the hand sharply down inwards and back up outwards in a sort of 0 shape.

In the case of one-handed grabs, the attacker will either release directly or be bent forwards leaving himself vulnerable and then letting go.

In case of a double grab the arms will when the technique is applied lock the attacker's arms when the hands point downwards, and the grip is released.

3. Wrist release two handed

("Wrist Release: Wrist Held by Two Hands" KMW Krav Maga Yellow belt curriculum. "One hand grabbed by two hands low holds " IKMF P3 Curriculum)

First grab your own hand from above, then proceed to pull it up towards yourself and bring the elbow of the pulled hand across. Your hand should now be free and in position to deliver a horizontal hammer fist (or chop) to the jaw, temple, or neck.

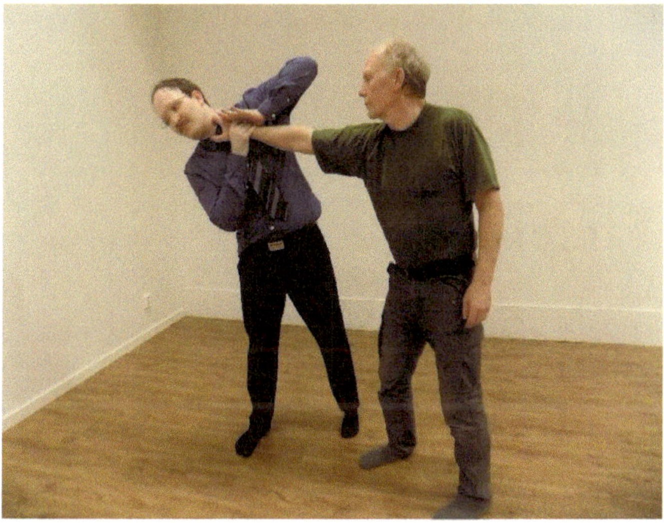

4. Standing elbow lock

(I think I first met this technique in Viking Cronholm´s Jiujitsu tricks but later also as “Waki Gatame” from the Ju-Jutsu Kais brown belt curriculum. and “Ude Hisigi Waki Gatame” technique number 5 of 10 under Kansetsu Waza in the Katame Waza section by Kodokan Judo)

Against one handed chokes, clothes grabs, and other attempted grabs and strangles.

Grab unto the attackers’ in this case right arm with your right arm closest to you. If your hands grip goes unto the attackers hand a bit that will assist the technique. bring your left elbow up and spin 180 degrees clockwise around. The attackers’ arm is now locked under your arm. Keep your weight on the elbow. From here you can bring him all the way to the ground, break the arm, perform other grappling moves or strike the attacker.

5 Strangle defence front

("Choke from Front with a Push" KMW Krav Maga yellow belt curriculum) If pushed backwards turn towards the rear foot. What ever the direction, bring the arm on the opposite side up to your ear and then as you rotate bring your elbow sharply down. (Immediately follow up with an elbow or punch).

6 Strangle defence rear

("Choke from Behind with a Push" KMW Krav Maga yellow belt curriculum) The same move can be applied against a strangle from behind. Again turn towards the rear foot if the feet are apart as from a push, in this version raise the arm on the same side.

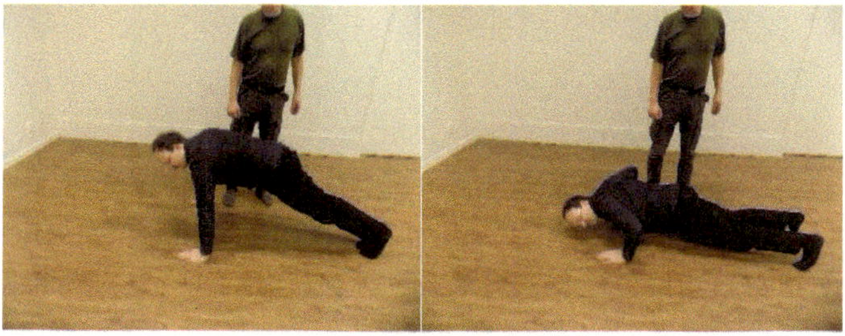

7. Forward break fall (IKMF Krav Maga)

Simply land into a push up, make sure to turn your head sideways. (Note that the arms flex and that if you are not strong enough to catch yourself it's ok to just slow yourself down to reduce impact and be careful not to break your wrists. Practice by doing pushups)

8. Backward break fall

("Back Fall Break" KMW Krav Maga Orange Curriculum and "Ushiro Ukemi" In Judo) As you fall backwards bring your head forwards away from the ground and smash the ground with straight arms at a roughly 45 degree angle, palms down.

Make sure to protect yourself as you stand up.

9. Side break fall

("Side Fall Break" in the KMW Krav Maga orange belt curriculum, "side break fall" in IKMF Krav Maga P3 curriculum and "Yoko Ukemi" in Judo)

When slipping or being tripped or thrown:

Land on the side with your arm straight at ca 45 degrees out striking the ground.

Divide the weight over the arm and leg, while allowing the other leg to remain bent. Do not put your elbow under yourself when falling or you may damage your shoulder. Always keep your head up of the ground. (This technique is highly valuable and one of the most likely to get use of)

To get up, Plant one hand and pull your legs in under yourself and stand up while guarding your head with the other.

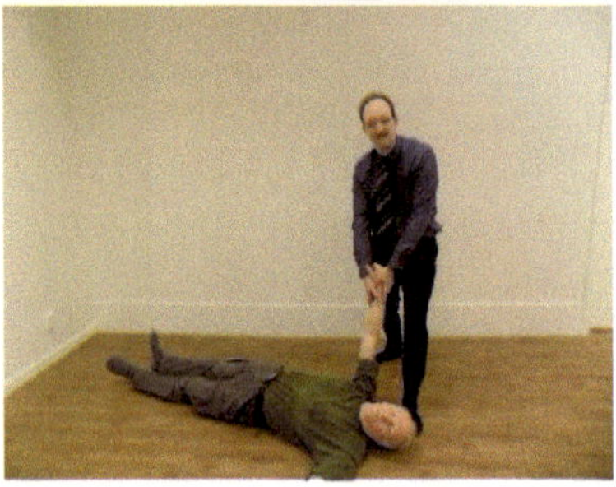

10. Hip throw

("Hip Throw" KMW Krav Maga brown belt curriculum. "O GOSHI" In JJK as technique 2 in the nage waza section of the green belt curriculum, and O-goshi as technique 2 in the Koshi-waza category in the Nage waza section of Kodokan Judo.)

This technique is useful to throw an attacker standing close to you and to practice your sideways falling technique. Step in and turn while grabbing around the attacker´s lower back with one arm and grabbing his wrist or arm with the other. Put your hip below the attackers' hip and using your weight pull the attacker unto your hip and over. (Remember to keep your head up when falling as practice partner. Always hold onto wrist as thrower to aid partner)

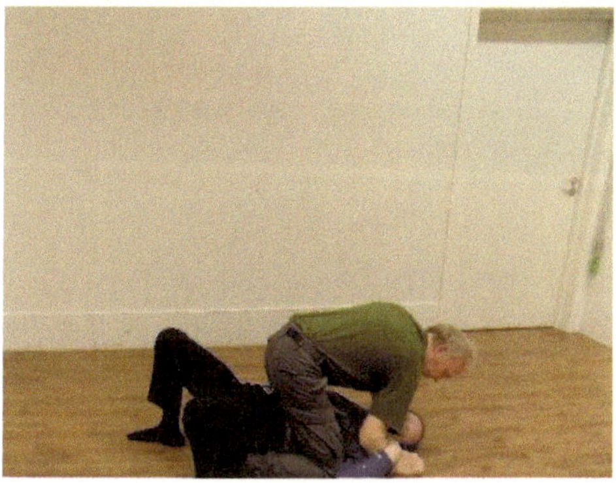

11. Ground mount escape

("Trap and Roll against Full Mount" (Wrap arm) "Choke with Attacker in mount" (Pluck arm) KMW Krav Maga in the orange belt curriculum. BJJ)

(In this picture I use the pull trap version but you can also try the arm wrap version where you wrap your arm around the attackers' arm from above)

As the attacker sits on you, buck your hips so the attacker has to catch himself with his arms. Put your left foot outside the attackers' right foot, and grab his right arm with your left arm and pull it in. (Or wrap your arm around it from above)

Then buck your hips again while pushing of with your right foot causing the attacker to fall as he has no way to catch himself.

You are now sitting by the feet. and can escape in a way appropriate for the situation.

Note that the groin may be within attacking range as you get up but watch out for the attackers' feet.

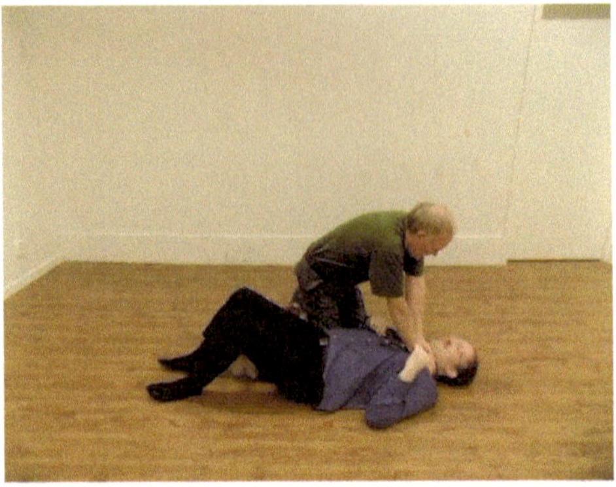

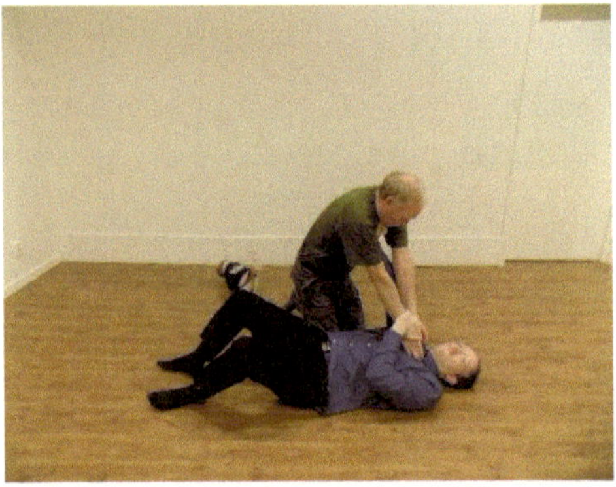

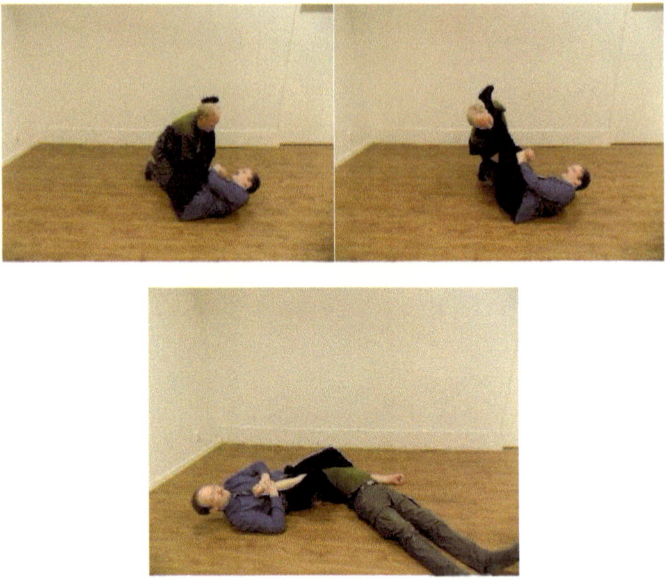

12. Ground strangle defence

(IKMF Krav Maga and "Choke from the Side Defence" KMW Krav Maga green belt curriculum)
When the attacker is sitting next to you strangling you, pull with the hand away from the attacker on the choke to relieve some pressure while with the other in this case right hand strikes with the fingers to the throat in order to create space for the knee nearest to the attacker. Use the knee to push him up and put your left foot in front of the attackers' face and kick as hard as you can. (Optionally put your leg over and bring the attackers head down, hold his hand tight to yourself and use your bodyweight to straighten the attackers' arm to the breaking point. Always be careful not to injure an opponent during training. If the attacker tries to bite you or similar break the arm and stand up. This Armbar is called Juji Gatame in Judo)

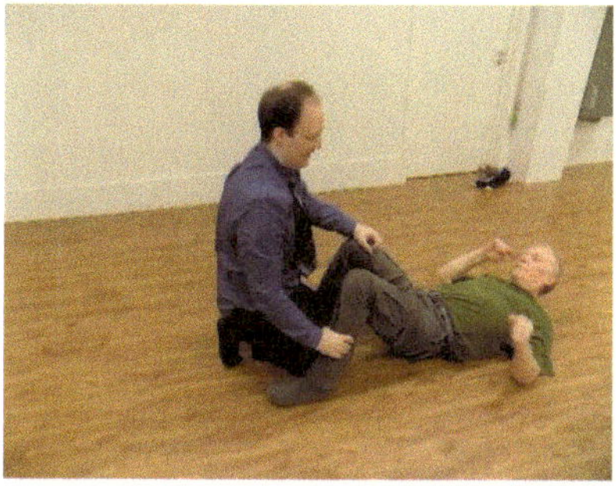

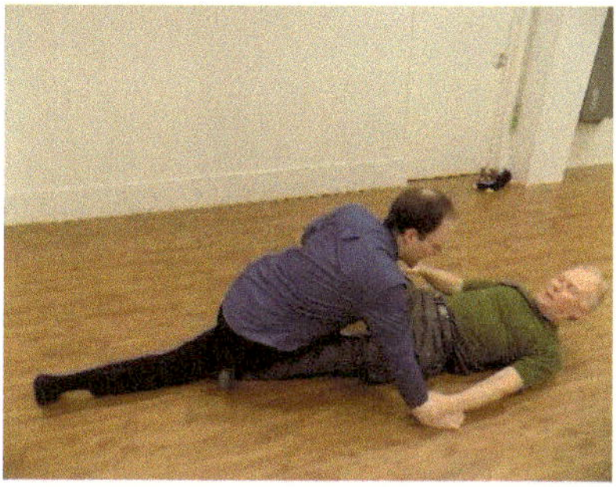

13. Ground between the knees escape

("STRYPTAG MOT LIGGANDE, sittande mellan benen frigörning" roughly translates to: choke against person laying down, sitting between the legs freeing/release/escape. Technique 12 of the Katame waza section in the orange belt curriculum

of Jujutsu Kai)

As the attacker sits between the legs:

Place your left foot on the attacker's right knee and kick it away in a stomping motion while holding onto his left arm to bring him down on his side. (Remember that you can use your knees to make space and that the head may be a target for kicks sometimes as well. Once free, run away.

(If you are too close scootch back and twist.)

(The opportunity may arise for an armbar or similar)

(This is originally against an attacker choking you from this position but can be applied for some other situations aswell.)

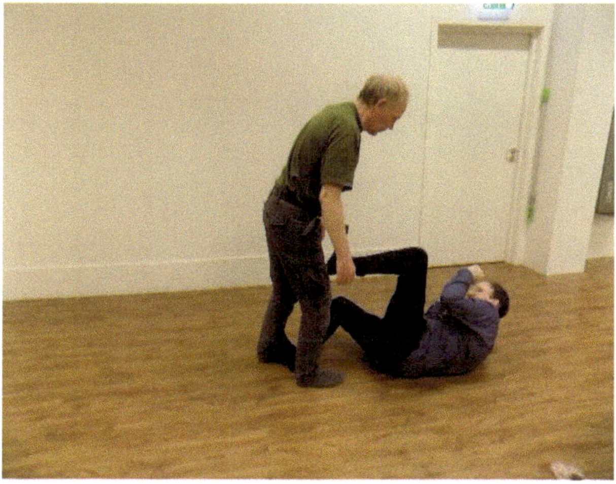

14. Ground defence position

("Side Position" KMW Krav Maga yellow belt curriculum)

Whenever on the ground and the attacker is not on you, yet is too close to get up safely, use the Ground defence position.

Keep one arm and one leg up, protect yourself with the arm and aim at any available body parts with the foot, such as groin, knees, or head etc depending on the situation. (You can lift your hips by planting the right foot and pushing of for increased reach)

You can also use this at some points during other techniques.

Don't forget to call for help, never freeze, always fight on until you are safe.

Get up as soon as it is safe to do so.

15. Palm strike (Optionally from active wedge guard.) (With or without eye poke and groin kick.)

(JJK “SHOTEI UCHI, jodan” from the Atemi waza section of the yellow belt curriculum, Defendu and KMW Krav Maga “Palm heel strike” yellow belt curriculum)

(Guard, I have seen multiple variations of this, and it’s used to protect against incoming flurries of strikes while changing distance.

In some variations one or both hands are wrapped around the back of the head, in others the hands are on top of the head or like in the KMW “defence against hook punch (covering)” the fist remains closed.)

First let's start with the palmstrike itself. Build to it all the way from the ground. Push off with your right foot as if to jump, rotate your hips and shoulders and strike with the heel (bony base) of the hand. The Fairbairn way to do it is: knee to the testicles and with the palm to the chin and fingers in the eyes forcing the persons head backwards while striking to the full extent of reach. (WE Fairbairn taught the Shanghai police and later OSS and military units in WWII as well as invented Defendu and the FS fighting knife) (If your knee doesn't reach snap your leg out bringing the shin to the groin)

Another possible target is the nose.

This is a close-range technique to get an attacker of yourself.

Next is the guard part. Place your arms in a V shape with your elbows pointing forwards towards the attacker's face to protect your head (Covers jaw and temple while deflecting high and low straights and if the punch lands on the elbow the attackers' hand may be damaged)

In order to protect your liver etc shoot the elbow down to the hip.

Now finally let´s put these together.

Create a wedge shape with one arm and palm strike (or Punch) with the other. When you do so you can bring your in this case right shoulder up to protect your jaw during the strike to further reduce the risk of getting knocked out, should the attacker try to punch you.

16. Defensive font kick

(Savate (Kunz and Pua) “Chasse frontal median” Green glove curriculum. KMW Krav Maga “Front Kick (Vertical Target)” yellow belt curriculum. IKMF Krav Maga “Defensive Forward Kick” P2 Curriculum.)

Raise your knee high and extend the leg in a sharp pushing motion towards the mid-section landing on either the ball or heel of the foot. Notice the right foot is turned out when kicking with the left foot. Use this to push an attacker back and if lucky bring him to the ground or to bend forward. (an alternate target to the stomach is the hip)

17. Stick: Vertical inside "Dive" defence

(Krav Maga variation, in KMW it's performed with a punch during the step in and followed by a knee, (Blue belt) other variations dive in, and there are many possible follow-ups including both throwing, and or striking)

For this defence "Dive" in with your hands close together and your arms almost but not quite straight. Put your right hand/arm on the attackers' shoulder to keep him off to the side. wrap your left arm from above around the attackers' arm that is holding the stick and bring it back up as a guard. Now with the stick locked you can, strike, throw or disarm the attacker.

To disarm the attacker, exaggerate the guard and turn away from the attacker. Then grab the lowest end of the stick and break it out. You now have a stick to strike with.

(The last disarm part I'm not sure where I got but it seems to work well enough)

18. Stick: Horizontal “Guard” defence

(Krav Maga hybrid variation based on defence against high round kicks (Green belt) and stick defence against of angle attacks (Blue belt))

Against horizontal strikes quickly step in and turn your body,

and let the opponent’s arm (or as far in on the stick as possible)

land on the two thirds of the guard closest to your elbows.

Then proceed to disarm the attacker by turning the stick towards the back of the attacker’s hand. (This can be done form a variety of positions, if you are not in such a position throwing or tripping the attacker may be an option. The further in on the stick you get, the less damage you receive from the attack. At a close range enough the stick becomes of little use)

19. Stick: Vertical outside “X” defence

(Krav Maga variation from KMW defence against of angle attacks in the blue belt curriculum, with a wraped arm from below instead of grabbed arm from above)

Meet the attackers in this case right arm or near hand part of stick with your right arm at an high angle as always.

Placeyour left hand under so you can lock the attackers arm to your body for a moment while your right hand slides out on the stick and twists it towards the back of the hand, thus out of it.

(Follow up as nessecary, just because you got past or even took away the stick doesn’t mean it’s over yet. Don’t stop until you have an opportunity to get away safely)

20. Knife: 360 defence

("360 Defence (Outside Defence)" from KMW yellow and brown belt curriculums. (and IKMF and KMG etc))

One of the most classic techniques of Krav Maga.

This technique works great against knife attacks from the outside such as stabs from below from the side or icepick stabs from above. Make sure to lean forward for the high and low version in order to create space between yourself and the arm as the knife blade may otherwise reach you anyways.

Always keep your arm at 90 degrees or just above, avoid protecting with your hand or wrist as it may be too weak. Use the forearm to defend, if the angle of the arm is too high during a high defence, then the knife may slide down and open your gut, if the angle is too high during a low defence the knife may slide up into your neck. If on the other hand the angle is too low the arm may fold in from the attack and fail to protect you. Practice plenty, and always strike simultaneously with the other hand as hard as you can.

(This can also be used in multiple other situations and with other objects as long as the attacks are from the outside (as opposed to straight at you) and relatively in close. Don't use it against heavy stick attacks as your arm may break)

21. Knife: Folds

(Hybrid of "Inside Defence against Straight Punch" (Yellow belt) and "Knife Defence against Straight Stab" (Brown belt) from KMW Krav Maga)

This technique works on a similar premise to the 360 but instead of meeting the attack you deflect it with an almost slapping motion while striking with the other hand. This is against straight stabs. Make sure to move the arms simultaneously. (If possible kick the attacker away instead. It may depending on circumstances be appropriate to follow this technique with a kick. Striking hard is important. Blinding the opponent by hand or object can help you get away in some situations. If objects are available around you use them as appropriate)

22. Knife: Standing elbow lock

(Jujutsu)

In this variation the elbow lock is used against an attacker with a sharp object. This is in case the object is being held to your body.

(Note, if the object is held to opposite side of the throat of where you are turning you will have to pull it sharply down first in order to not exectute yourself)

23. Gun: Long front defence

(“Gun from the front” from KMW Krav Maga blue belt curriculum)

I tend to favour this technique. It jams the gun and works from a relatively longer distance.

With your left hand assuming a right-handed attacker, grab the gun tightly while redirecting it in order to make the first bullet miss and jam the second. Push the gun firmly to the attackers’ stomach and keep it there as the attacker may otherwise bring you back into the line of fire by stepping backwards, simultaneously punch with all your weight to the face or solar plexus. Next grab the gun with your right hand by the back at the hammer area from below. Twist it 180 degrees counterclockwise to open the attackers grip, potentially damaging his fingers (obs careful in training, keep your finger of the trigger for the latter part of this technique) then turn it 90 degrees back while pulling to get it out of his hand (kick to the balls if needed) and into your own hand. You now have the gun in your hand, reload to unjam and fire at the attackers legs so he can’t follow as you run away. Hand the firearm in to the appropriate authorities.)

24. Gun: Close front defence

(Hybrid Krav Maga)

This technique was favoured by a retired police officer who was a part of one of the tests because of its simple easy to remember mechanics. (The downside is that the gun is not disabled until further into the technique that is slightly slower)

Grab the wrist from above with in this case the left hand and push it right while turning your entire body clockwise. Next grab the gun from underneath and rotate your body back, breaking the gun out of the hand. (Can also be done from the side to protect a third party)

25. Gun: quick front defence

(Origin unknown but probably Krav Maga of some kind) This technique is favoured by my father. (It depends on speed and the full technique is completed in but a second. The downside is that it is a little more technical and requires more practice) The left hand (assuming a right handed attacker) grabs the gun pushing it right and up then left and up, while the right hand strikes to the wrist thus facilitating the dissarm where left hand pushes forwards over the attackers right arm coming down on the outside of it. The way the gun is held after dissarming it allows you to rapidly place it in your own hand. (Keep in mind gun dissarms should come as a surprise. If somebody is robbing you just give them the money and call the authorities. If someone is taking hostages or walking around executing people, attempting a gun defence may be warrented. Be aware that there are always risks in defending against guns)

26. Gun: Back defence

("Gun from Behind (Touching)" KMW Krav Maga from the blue belt curriculum)

Turn inward and pluck the gun arm, squeezing it between the lower and upper arm.

Grab unto the attackers' neck from your own side and kick with your knee or shin as appropriate to the situation.

Finally grab the gun and break it towards the back of the hand, out of the hand.

(You can then use it to strike the attacker before backing off and readying the gun.)

Training

There is enough to say about mitts for a book of its own. So I will just tell you what you need to know to stay safe.

If training strikes with mitts:

As partner: do not put your hands in front of your face as you will get the mitts in your face, or far out above your shoulders as this may result in injury to your shoulders.

Keep your hands slightly apart and away from your face. Always keep your wrists straight to avoid injury. (If you need to get lower bend your knees, never your wrists)

(You can number strikes and call them out 1&2 Jab & Cross, 3&4 Lead hook & Rear hook, 5&6 Lead uppercut & Rear uppercut. If swiping at the puncher for him/her to bob under keep the mitt at a 45-degree angle so if the puncher fails, the puncher doesn't get hit by the edge but the flat of the mitt that then bounces off safely. (Later on, you can learn about the details of how to do it well)

As puncher: Rotate your body for stronger strikes, land on your top two knuckles and always keep your wrists straight. Also don't forget to keep your guard up and stand with the feet about shoulder-width apart and one foot a step forward.

To strike hard become stronger, practice push-ups, bag striking, planks, sit-ups, walking lunges and running. Also, if you have a gym nearby, put those machines and weights to good use.

Beginners should always be thrown/ fall unto a soft surface.

Consider your surroundings and practice carefully so as to not injure your training partner.

If instructing:

it's important to put an emphasis on safety first. Make sure there are no unnecessarily dangerous practices and find out if anyone has a health condition.

Keep in mind that students may also be suffering from trauma. Don't assume that they are going to be ok with what ever you usually do. Say what's going to happen before it happens and check that they are ok with each step and encourage them to speak out if they are not comfortable with the situation and adapt accordingly as needed.
(Obviously also respect their privacy when it comes to any information they may choose to share)

Leave prestige and ego behind and keep a positive attitude.

Mini HIIT

A starting program, kind to beginners at the end of the training, or at home.

1. Butt kicks
2. Knee thrusts
3. Punches
4. Speed bag
5. Climbers
6. Plank jacks
7. Toe tap Crunches
8. Uppercuts
9. Behind the back jacks
10. Jog in place.

Each exercise is carried out at high intensity for 20 seconds followed by 10 seconds rest before the next.

The full program is performed twice.

Thus, the full training is 10 min.

1.Butt kicks

Jog in place while trying to kick your own butt with your heels.

2.Knee thrusts

Bring your hands together high as if to grab an attacker

and thrust your knee high. (It's knee thrusts, not knee lifts.)

3.Punches

Stand with your feet shoulder-width apart and strike as quickly as you can at an imaginary target in front of you.

4.Speed bag

Just as it sounds strike an imaginary speedbag with your hands fast.

5.Climbers

From a plank (The position of a push up) Bring a leg up towards your arm and place it back and then alternate sides.

6.Plank jacks

Stand in the Plank, Jump your feet apart then back together.

7.Toe tap Crunches

Hold your arms straight up then bring them down in front of you straight out, at the same time lift a leg in a fast-thrusting manner until your toes touches your fingertips, alternate between right and left sides.

8.Uppercuts

When performing them turn your body so you throw your right uppercut to the left and left to the right

9.Behind the back jacks

As a regular jumping jack except clapping behind your back and above your head.

10. Jog in place.

As it sounds.

ESD

The principles of ESD (Empowerment self-defense) are:

1. Think

(access the situation)

2. Yell

(Set boundaries, be assertive)

3. Run

(Or leave, or ask someone else to leave)

4. Fight

(Using self-defence techniques along with loud NO! yells or other verbal boundaries such as back off! to get an attacker away and bring attention from others to the situation)

5. Tell

(Make sure there is someone you can talk to if something happens)

Dr Jocelyn A. Hollander PhD. Department of Sociology, University of Oregon.

“Women who complete an ESD course are both more likely to avoid rape if targeted and less likely to be targeted in the first place”.

About ESD:

“Teaches effective physical tactics that requires minutes or hours rather than years to learn and can be adapted for any body”.

• • •

Resistance does on average does not increase risk of injury.

(7 Publications support this)

ESD training reduces women’s risk of assault.

(6 major studies and 10 publications support this)

ESD training can stop assault

(5 publications support this)

• • •

According to statistics from publications above both risk of rape or assault and completion thereof are roughly cut in half by ESD training.

You can learn more from the University of Oregon.

Krav Maga principles

1. Neutralize the Threat

(Act decisively to neutralize the threat promptly.)

2. Avoid, Prevent, and De-escalate

(Whenever possible, aim to avoid dangerous situations.)

3. Inflict Maximum Damage, Sustain Minimum Harm

(prioritize delivering powerful strikes to the attacker while minimizing harm to yourself.)

4. Prioritize Third-Party Protection

(When defending others, prioritize the safety of your loved ones at all costs.)

5. Act Within the Law

(Adhere to the law while implementing Krav Maga techniques.)

Use note

The techniques selected here are chosen for versatility and ease of learning. For all of an average build.

The relevant scenarios where various techniques may be useful include but are not necessarily limited to:

Domestic violence,

Violence in the workplace,

Unexpected assault,

And escaping bar brawls,

As well as a few weapon techniques that may be suitable for:

Security guards,

Police officers,

And individuals living in dangerous areas.

In a verbal confrontation, deescalate when possible,

Against a socially forceful individual, be assertive but calm.

Confidence reduces chance of attack. (both in speech and movement, as criminals etc like easy targets)

Helpful phrases include but are not limited to direct phrases like: No! Go away! Back off! And assertive phrases like:

This is how it is, The rules say… and Now!

(more about de-escalation will not fit in this booklet but is available elsewhere)

Legal note

***Weapons** techniques are very risky as is everything in a very violent confrontation. The more you practice the better is your chance, however there are no guarantees and a move that fails or is performed in the wrong circumstance or with the wrong timing can lead to serious injury or death. Only attempt these as a last resort, well aware of what you are risking and with the full understanding that the results there of be they positive or negative are solely your own responsibility. (This also goes for all training)*

***Levels of violence** are at your discretion ranging from a simple standing armbar or wrist release along with a phrase like No! or Alright don't do anything you will regret, take it easy. In lower threat situation to potentially lethal violence in higher threat situations. This booklet can not foresee the exact circumstances of your situation and it is thus up to you to determine the appropriate response and to take full responsibility for your actions, that should be reasonably defendable in a court of law, and to your own conscience.*

***Self-defence** techniques here shown are classics known to work well. However, in a real situation there are many variables and you don't know what the other person knows or is capable of. In self-defence as in all fighting and violence there are no guarantees and it is up to you to use good judgment and to know your limits.*

***Responsibility** is solely your own and not shared by the author, any organisation or any individual associated with this booklet. This is both in regard to techniques, safe practice, real life use and law, and any other aspect.*

Scenarios and options

The ***wrist releases*** *are probably most likely needed in either a domestic situation, a situation of unwanted attention turning forceful out in a club or bar etc, or if someone attempts to pull you along into for an example van or some bushes for the purposes of kidnappings or other atrocities. Use the release to free yourself and get away.*

The ***standing elbow lock*** *can also be used as an option to the front strangle defence, it is versatile and can also be used when someone is trying to grab you, your belongings, strangling a third party, holding a weapon to you or is pushing you aswell as it original purpose against one handed strangles. It also allows for a softer option should you wish to try and not harm the attacker. Another useful feture is the multiple finish options including taking the person to the ground, putting them on a bar or table, turning back to trip, throw or push them, breaking the arm, or striking them. It can also in some situations be used to pin them to the ground. Thus useful in a situation of escalating violence or a domestic situation. The option of* ***strangle defences*** *can be used both standing, while being pushed and against a wall, another option to these are to strike to the eyes or if you can reach to punch the attacker as his guard is away during the strangle leaving him vulnerable.*

Breakfalls *are probably the most likely to be used in real life. They protect you in a variety of situations including being pushed, tripped, thrown, or slipping on for an example ice, wet floor or by missing a step. I once lived in a building with smooth stone stairs that would get very slippery when wet in the fall and spring. At least twice I fell down those stairs. Thanks to proper falling technique I was able to dust myself off and continue my day without injuries.*

The ***hip throw*** *is useful when one has ended up to close to for an example a drunkard at the bar blocking the way and acting violently, it can be performed nicely by letting the person down carefully making sure they don't hurt themselves as in practice. Or in a dangerous situation you hit them with the earth and knock them out or worse by dropping them on their head. The hip throw is however in here for another reason as well, it provides good opportunity to practice the side breakfall. In addition, it can be used in some other situations such as during a failing stick disarm attempt.*

The ***ground techniques*** *are selected to facilitate escape during violent encounters. While women are the main audience for these techniques they can end up being useful for others as well, if for an example you are suddenly tackled to the ground by an attacker trying to beat you. The ground is a place to avoid especially if you are not an experienced grappler. (but also because there may be dangerous objects or circumstances coming into play). The mount defence while useful is a dangerous thing, an experienced grappler may counter it or you may get panicked or knocked out before completing the move. The side strangle defence is likely a domestic situation rather than assault outside, it comes with two finishing options, a kick to get the attacker away and an armbar option. Note that the armbar option in this case may not be soft option as the attackers head will get slammed towards the hard floor. The between the knees defence offers a way to cause the attacker to fall to the side and is mainly for a situation where the attacker is leaning forward to strangle or grab you (probably during an attempt of SA in the home or out) however this technique can also work for more upright positions. Should the attacker be so heavy or so positioned as to not move, push anyway so hard that you move yourself back, as you then place yourself in a position to kick, this is an option for that circumstance.*

The ***palm strike*** *is useful in that it pushes an attacker away from you as you strike. Options are to push an attacker with both hands if he is not holding you. Or to increase potential damage and reach while having a longer distance and lacking some of the pushing effect by using a closed fist. The movement can also be used in different ways with fingers to the eyes or simply striking the nose. The scenarios where this technique is useful may include against forceful advances by a man, in the home or elsewhere, or to create the space to escape while someone is striking you or blocking your escape route. It can also be used together with the* ***wedge guard****. This guard fills two purposes and is the option to two other classic approaches. First it allows you to close the distance if needed against someone striking you, simply ram you way into them like a battering ram. From there you can then push them away, palm strike them, elbow them, knee them, trip them or throw them, as is appropriate to the situation. The other purpose is to prevent knockout during an assault with fists, thus facilitating either escape or the use of the palm strike or punch in order to create the needed space to escape. The other two options are parries and slips, as they require longer training I'm not featuring them here. The* ***front kick*** *is mainly to create space in order to allow you to take other actions, or grab items.*

Stick techniques *are all about closing the distane. However in an actual altercation where bullies etc may be beating you disarming can sometimes prove tricky. If that is the case you have other options. Those include Throwing the attacker to the ground, tripping the attacker, striking or eye poking the attacker as a distraction, or in some cases attempting a different disarm. Weapon techniques tend to require more training and skills than the basic defence techniques.*

Knife techniques *are here designed to create space between yourself and the attacker, well used together with the front kick it can create the pace necessary to allow an officer or guard to draw is firearm or taser, but also allow a civilian to grab a chair, bottle, pool cue, sharp object, or other suitable tool for self-defence.*

Gun defence *is meant for kidnaping/hostage situations and school shootings etc. (Against a robbery it's usually safer to just hand over the money)*

In conclusion this booklet is designed to give you basic tools for a variety of situations to help keep you safe.

Thank you.

Books other than this little booklet....

For further self-defence techniques:

Complete Krav Maga ISBN: 978-1-56975-573-0 / 9781612435589

Or for just punches and kicks:

Savate Assaut and Combat ISBN: 9781387859085

Special thanks to: Hälsostudion Skara

(Local gym in Skara)

and

Tasha Ina Church

(Founder of ElleLiveAction with over 20 years martial arts experience and certified ESD coach)

"Empowerment Self-Defense is a necessity, something everyone can benefit from. It goes beyond physical moves to encompass verbal self-defense, boundary setting, de-escalation and so much more! I read Adam Ivehags Booklet and loved what he had to say about ESD! We need more Adams in the world spreading the word about this work. His visuals were helpful to understand the material! As someone with 24 years in this field, I found what he had to say about empowerment self-defense helpful and on point! It is definitely worth a read!"

Author: Adam Ivehag

MIX

Papper från ansvarsfulla källor
Paper from responsible sources

FSC® C105338

© 2024 Adam Ivehag
Publisher: BoD • Books on Demand, Stockholm, Sverige
Print: Libri Plureos GmbH, Hamburg, Tyskland
ISBN: 978-91-8080-108-9